WHY DO WE FAIL?

"FAILURE IS A NATURAL PART OF THE LEARNING PROCESS, AND IT IS OFTEN THROUGH OUR FAILURES THAT WE GROW AND LEARN THE MOST"

UDESHYA SINGH

Made with ♥ on the Notion Press Platform
www.notionpress.com

To all those who have experienced failure and have felt the sting of disappointment and frustration, this book is for you. May you find comfort and inspiration in the words written within these pages, and may you be reminded that failure is not the end, but rather a stepping stone on the path to success.

Contents

Foreword *vii*

Preface *ix*

Acknowledgements *xi*

Prologue *xiii*

1. Lack Of Effort Or Preparation 1

2. Fear Of Failure 8

3. Lack Of Focus 18

4. External Factor 21

5. Negative Self-talk 29

Conclusion 35

FOREWORD

We often hear about the successes of others - the stories of triumph, victory, and achievement. But what about the stories of failure? The experiences that shape us, humble us, and teach us invaluable lessons?

In **"Why Do We Fail?"**, the author explores the complex and multifaceted nature of failure - from the factors beyond our control to the self-imposed limitations we place on ourselves. Through a thoughtful and reflective examination of the different types of failures that individuals and organizations encounter, the author provides insight into how we can overcome the obstacles that stand in our way.

This book is a reminder that failure is not something to be feared, but rather an opportunity for growth and learning. It is a testament to the resilience of the human spirit, and a guide for those who seek to overcome the challenges they face.

I am honored to introduce this book and recommend it to anyone who has ever experienced failure, or who wishes to understand the complexities of the journey towards success.

Udeshya Singh

FOREWORD

[illegible]

PREFACE

Failure is an integral part of the human experience. Whether we like it or not, we will all encounter setbacks and disappointments in our lives. However, it is not the failure itself that defines us, but rather how we respond to it.

In writing this book, I have sought to explore the many different aspects of failure - from the external factors that are beyond our control, to the internal barriers that we erect for ourselves. Through research, personal experience, and the stories of others, I have sought to provide insight into the many different ways that failure can impact us, and how we can learn from our mistakes to ultimately achieve success.

This book is not a prescription for success, nor is it a guide for how to avoid failure. Instead, it is a celebration of the journey - of the many ups and downs, twists and turns, and unexpected detours that we encounter along the way. It is a reminder that failure is not something to be ashamed of, but rather an opportunity to learn, grow, and become the best version of ourselves.

I hope that this book will inspire and encourage all those who read it to embrace failure as an essential part of the human experience, and to approach their lives with a sense of resilience, optimism, and perseverance.

Udeshya Singh

PREFACE

[illegible] is an integral part of the human experience. Whether we like it or not, we will all encounter [illegible] and [illegible] in our lives. However, it is not the [illegible] itself that defines us but rather how we respond to [illegible]

[illegible]

ACKNOWLEDGEMENTS

Writing a book is never a solitary endeavor, and this project would not have been possible without the support and contributions of many individuals.

First and foremost, I would like to express my gratitude to my family, who have been my constant source of encouragement and support throughout this journey. Thank you for always believing in me and pushing me to pursue my dreams.

I would also like to thank my friends and colleagues, who have offered invaluable feedback, insights, and inspiration along the way. Your perspectives and experiences have enriched this book immeasurably.

To the experts and scholars whose research and writing have informed and inspired my own, thank you for your dedication and contributions to the field of psychology, personal development, and success.

I am also indebted to the publishers, editors, designers, and other professionals who have worked tirelessly to bring this book to life. Thank you for your expertise, creativity, and attention to detail.

Finally, I would like to express my deep appreciation to the readers of this book, who have taken the time to engage with my ideas and insights. I hope that this book has been a source of inspiration and guidance, and that it has helped you to embrace failure as a vital part of the journey to success.

Thank you.

Udeshya Singh

Prologue

Failure is an inevitable part of life. Whether it is a small setback or a major disappointment, we have all experienced the bitter taste of failure at some point in our lives. However, the way we respond to failure is what defines us. Do we give up and walk away, or do we use our failures as a catalyst for growth and success?

In this book, we explore the various factors that contribute to failure, both internal and external. From fear of failure to lack of preparation, we examine the different obstacles that can stand in the way of our success. Through real-life examples and practical advice, we learn how to overcome these challenges and build resilience in the face of adversity.

The journey towards success is not easy, and failure is an inevitable part of that journey. But by understanding why we fail and how we can overcome it, we can turn our failures into stepping stones towards a brighter future.

I

Lack Of Effort or Preparation

Lack of effort or preparation is a common problem that many individuals face in their personal and professional lives. Whether it is studying for an exam, preparing for a work presentation, or simply keeping up with daily responsibilities, the lack of effort or preparation can have serious consequences. In this article, we will explore the reasons behind this phenomenon and offer tips to overcome it.

Reasons for lack of effort or preparation

There are many reasons why people may struggle with putting in the necessary effort or preparation. Here are some of the most common reasons:

Procrastination: Procrastination is a common problem for many people. It is the act of delaying or putting off tasks until the last minute. This often results in a lack of effort or preparation because there is not enough time to properly prepare.

Lack of motivation: Another reason why people may struggle with effort or preparation is a lack of motivation. When someone is not motivated to do something, they are less likely to put in the necessary effort or preparation.Poor time management: Poor time management skills can also contribute to a lack of effort or preparation. When someone does not manage their time effectively, they may not have enough time to prepare adequately for a task.

Overconfidence: Sometimes, people may feel overconfident in their abilities and underestimate the amount of effort or preparation required for a task. This can lead to a lack of effort or preparation and poor results.

Tips to overcome lack of effort or preparation

If you are struggling with a lack of effort or preparation, here are some tips to help you overcome it:

Set clear goals: Setting clear goals can help you stay focused and motivated. Make sure your goals are specific, measurable, achievable, relevant, and time-bound (SMART).

Break tasks into smaller steps: Breaking tasks into smaller steps can make them feel more manageable and less overwhelming. This can help you stay motivated and on track.

Use a planner or calendar: Using a planner or calendar can help you manage your time more effectively. Make sure you schedule time for preparation and stick to your schedule.

Eliminate distractions: Distractions can make it difficult to focus and can lead to a lack of effort or preparation. Try to eliminate distractions by turning off your phone or finding a quiet place to work.

Hold yourself accountable: Hold yourself accountable by setting deadlines and regularly checking in on your progress. You can also find an accountability partner to help keep you on track.

Practice self-discipline: Self-discipline is the ability to control your impulses and stay focused on your goals. It takes practice, but the more you practice self-discipline, the easier it will become.

Conclusion

A lack of effort or preparation can have serious consequences in both personal and professional settings. By understanding the reasons behind this phenomenon and using the tips outlined above, you can overcome this problem and achieve the success you desire. Remember, it takes time and effort to develop good habits, but the results are worth it.

In today's fast-paced and ever-changing job market, it is essential to continuously develop your skills and knowledge to stay competitive and advance in your career. However, many individuals may fail to invest the necessary time and effort to develop the skills and knowledge required for their job. In this article, we will discuss the importance of developing skills and knowledge, the reasons why people may fail to do so, and how to overcome these challenges.

Lack of effort or preparation can have negative consequences in many aspects of life, including education, work, relationships, and personal development. When we fail to put in the necessary effort or preparation, we may not be able to achieve our goals, reach our full potential, or meet the expectations of others. In the context of education, lack of effort or preparation can lead to poor grades, missed deadlines, incomplete assignments, and a lack of understanding of key concepts. This can have long-term consequences, such as limited career options, difficulty in getting into a good university or graduate program, and reduced earning potential. In the workplace, lack of effort or preparation can lead to poor job performance, missed deadlines, incomplete projects, and a lack of professional growth. This can result in missed opportunities for promotion, decreased job security, and a damaged reputation.

In relationships, lack of effort or preparation can lead to misunderstandings, conflicts, and a lack of intimacy. This can result in feelings of dissatisfaction, unhappiness, and even the breakdown of the relationship. In terms of personal development, lack of effort or preparation can prevent us from reaching our full potential, achieving our goals, and living a fulfilling life. It can also lead to feelings of frustration, self-doubt, and regret. Overall, it is important to recognize the importance of effort and preparation in achieving success in all aspects of life.

By setting goals, creating a plan, and putting in the necessary effort and preparation, we can overcome obstacles and achieve our desired outcomes. Fixing a lack of effort or preparation requires a deliberate and sustained effort to change behavior and habits.

Here are some strategies that can be helpful in addressing this issue: Set clear and realistic goals: Identify what you want to achieve and set clear, achievable goals that are specific, measurable, and time-bound. Create a plan: Develop a plan that outlines the steps you need to take to achieve your goals. This can include breaking down your goals into smaller tasks, setting deadlines for each task, and identifying the resources you need to succeed.

Build accountability: Share your goals and plan with someone else who can hold you accountable for making progress. This could be a friend, family member, or coach.

Prioritize your time: Make sure to allocate time and energy to the tasks and activities that will help you achieve your goals. Avoid distractions and focus on what is most important. Develop a growth mindset: Embrace the idea that effort and preparation lead to growth and success. View challenges as opportunities for learning and improvement, rather than as obstacles to be avoided.

Seek support: Don't be afraid to seek out support and resources to help you achieve your goals. This could include a mentor, coach, therapist, or support group. Celebrate your successes: Recognize and celebrate your progress and achievements along the way. This can help motivate you to continue making progress and build momentum towards your goals. Remember that changing behavior and habits takes time and effort, but with persistence and commitment, it is possible to overcome a lack of effort or preparation and achieve success. Fixing our daily behavior can be challenging, as it often requires breaking old habits and forming new ones. Here are some common challenges we may face when trying to change our behavior:

Resistance to change: It can be difficult to break out of our comfort zones and embrace new behaviors. We may feel resistant to change or anxious about the unknown. Lack of motivation: It can be hard to stay motivated and committed to changing our behavior, particularly if we don't see immediate results. Lack of support: It can be difficult to change our behavior if we don't have the support of others. This could include friends, family members, or colleagues who may not understand or value our efforts. External stressors: Life can be unpredictable, and external stressors such as work demands, family responsibilities, and health issues can make it challenging to prioritize behavior change. Old habits die hard: Habits are deeply ingrained in our daily lives and can be difficult to break. We may find ourselves reverting back to old habits out of habit or familiarity.

Unrealistic expectations; It's important to set realistic expectations for behavior change. If our goals are too ambitious, we may feel discouraged if we don't see immediate progress. Lack of self-awareness: It can be challenging to identify the behaviors we need to change in order to achieve our goals. We may not be aware of our own patterns and tendencies. Overcoming these challenges requires self-reflection, self-discipline, and a willingness to seek support and guidance when needed. It's important to be patient with ourselves and celebrate small wins along the way. With persistence and effort, we can make positive changes to our daily behavior and improve our lives. Persistence and effort are key ingredients to changing our behavior and improving our daily lives. Here are some ways in which persistence and effort can lead to positive changes:

Breaking old habits: Old habits can be difficult to break, but with persistence and effort, we can gradually replace them with new, healthier behaviors. By consistently making an effort to practice new behaviors, we can establish new habits and routines that become second nature. Developing discipline: Changing our behavior often requires discipline and self-control. By persistently working towards our goals and staying focused on our priorities, we can strengthen our ability to resist temptation and make healthy choices.

Overcoming obstacles: Persistence and effort help us to push through obstacles and setbacks. We may encounter challenges or face setbacks along the way, but by persisting in our efforts, we can overcome these obstacles and continue making progress. Building momentum: When we consistently put effort into changing our behavior, we can build momentum towards our goals. Each small step we take can build on the previous one, leading to significant progress over time.

Achieving success: Ultimately, persistence and effort can lead to success in achieving our goals and improving our daily lives. By consistently putting in the effort to make positive changes, we can see the results of our efforts and feel a sense of accomplishment. It's important to note that persistence and effort require time and patience. Changing our behavior and improving our daily lives is a process that takes time and effort. By consistently putting in the effort and staying focused on our goals, we can create lasting change and improve our lives in meaningful ways.

II

Fear of Failure

Fear of failure is a powerful obstacle in success because it can hold individuals back from taking risks and pursuing their goals. When individuals are afraid of failing, they may avoid taking action or taking risks, which can prevent them from achieving their full potential.

Here are some ways In which fear of failure can hinder success:

Limits growth and development: When individuals are afraid of failing, they may avoid taking on new challenges or tasks that are outside of their comfort zone. This can limit their personal and professional growth and development and prevent them from acquiring new skills and knowledge.

Hinders creativity: Fear of failure can also hinder creativity, as individuals may feel hesitant to explore new ideas or approaches for fear of making mistakes. This can limit their ability to innovate and find new solutions to problems. Reduces motivation: Fear of failure can also reduce motivation, as individuals may feel demotivated or discouraged by the prospect of failure. This can make it harder for them to stay committed to their goals and persist in the face of setbacks.

Leads to missed opportunities: When individuals are afraid of failing, they may hesitate or avoid taking action, which can lead to missed opportunities. This can prevent them from achieving their goals and pursuing new opportunities that could lead to success. To overcome fear of failure and achieve success, individuals may need to reframe their mindset and adopt a growth mindset, in which they view failure as an opportunity for learning and growth. They may also benefit from setting realistic goals, breaking tasks into smaller, more manageable pieces, and seeking support or guidance when needed.

Finally, practicing self-compassion and positive self-talk can help individuals build their confidence and reduce their fear of failure, which can ultimately lead to greater success. When an individual limits their growth and development, it can lead to failure in several ways: Lack of skill development: If an individual avoids taking on new challenges or tasks outside of their comfort zone, they may miss out on opportunities to develop new skills and abilities.

This can leave them ill-equipped to handle future challenges and may lead to failure in their personal or professional life.

Stagnation: When an individual is not growing or developing, they may become stagnant and stuck in their current position or situation. This can prevent them from reaching their full potential and achieving their goals, which can lead to a sense of failure or disappointment. Inability to adapt: In today's fast-paced world, it's important to be able to adapt to new situations and challenges. If an individual is not actively developing their skills and knowledge, they may struggle to adapt to changes in their personal or professional life, which can lead to failure.

Missed opportunities: When an individual limits their growth and development, they may miss out on opportunities that could lead to success. For example, they may pass up on a job opportunity because they don't have the required skills, or they may miss out on a chance to collaborate on a project because they don't have the necessary knowledge. To avoid these potential failures, it's important for individuals to prioritize their growth and development. This may involve taking on new challenges, seeking out learning opportunities, and embracing new experiences. By continually growing and developing, individuals can become more adaptable, skilled, and resilient, which can ultimately lead to greater success and fulfillment in their personal and professional lives. Exploring new ideas and approaches is essential for personal and professional growth. Hesitating to try new things due to fear of making mistakes can hold us back and prevent us from reaching our full potential.

Here are a few reasons why we need to overcome our fear of making mistakes and embrace new ideas and approaches:

Innovation and progress: Trying new things and exploring new ideas is essential for innovation and progress. Without new ideas and approaches, we would be stuck doing things the same way, and progress would stagnate.

Learning and development: Making mistakes is an inevitable part of the learning process. By trying new things, we learn what works and what doesn't work, and we gain valuable experience that can help us improve and grow.

Overcoming obstacles: Trying new things can help us overcome obstacles and find new solutions to problems. When we are open to new ideas and approaches, we are more likely to find creative solutions to the challenges we face.

Building confidence: Trying new things can help build our confidence and self-esteem. When we take risks and try new things, we prove to ourselves that we are capable of achieving more than we thought possible. Overall, we need to embrace new ideas and approaches and not be hesitant to try new things. Making mistakes is a natural part of the learning process, and it is through mistakes that we learn and grow. By being open to new ideas and approaches, we can foster innovation, progress, and personal and professional development.

Fear of failure can reduce motivation in several ways:

Paralysis: When an individual is consumed with fear of failure, they may become paralyzed and unable to take action. This can lead to procrastination and avoidance of tasks or activities that they perceive as risky or challenging. Self-doubt: Fear of failure can cause individuals to doubt their abilities and question whether they are capable of succeeding. This can lead to a lack of confidence and motivation, as they may feel that their efforts will be futile. Negative thinking: Fear of failure can lead to negative thinking patterns, such as catastrophizing and focusing on the potential negative outcomes. This can be demotivating and lead to a sense of hopelessness.

Avoidance: When an individual is afraid of failing, they may avoid situations or activities that could lead to failure. This can limit their opportunities for growth and development, as well as reduce their motivation to take on new challenges. Fear of failure can often lead to perfectionism because individuals who are afraid of failing may feel that they need to be perfect in order to avoid making mistakes or experiencing failure. Perfectionism can be defined as a tendency to set unrealistically high standards for oneself and to engage in overly critical self-evaluation.

Perfectionism can be a coping mechanism for those who are afraid of failure, as it allows them to focus on achieving a perfect outcome rather than facing the potential for failure. However, this mindset can be problematic because it can lead to a number of negative consequences, such as anxiety, procrastination, and low self-esteem. When individuals are focused on being perfect, they may be less likely to take risks or try new things, as they are afraid of making mistakes or not meeting their own high standards. This can limit their opportunities for growth and development, as well as hinder their ability to learn from their mistakes and failures.

Overall, fear of failure can lead to perfectionism because individuals may believe that perfection is the only way to avoid failure. However, this mindset can be limiting and harmful, and it is important to develop a growth mindset that allows for learning from mistakes and failures. Fear of failure can cause individuals to doubt their abilities and question themselves because it can create a negative internal dialogue that undermines their confidence and self-esteem. When individuals are afraid of failing, they may begin to question whether they are capable of succeeding, which can lead to self-doubt and negative self-talk.

For example, if someone is afraid of failing an exam, they may begin to doubt their ability to learn and understand the material, even if they have performed well in the past. This negative internal dialogue can be self-perpetuating, leading to further anxiety and self-doubt, which can undermine their motivation and ability to succeed. Fear of failure can also lead to a fixed mindset, where individuals believe that their abilities are fixed and cannot be improved. This mindset can lead to a lack of motivation to learn and grow, as individuals may believe that failure is a reflection of their innate abilities rather than a normal part of the learning process.

Fear of failure can cause individuals to doubt their abilities and question themselves because it creates a negative internal dialogue that undermines their confidence and self-esteem. It is important to develop a growth mindset and practice self-compassion to overcome these negative thought patterns and maintain a positive sense of self-worth. Overall, fear of failure can reduce motivation by causing individuals to avoid taking action, doubt their abilities, engage in negative thinking, and limit their opportunities for growth and development.

To overcome this fear, individuals can work on developing a growth mindset, embracing failure as a learning opportunity, and setting realistic goals that focus on progress rather than perfection. Additionally, seeking support from friends, family, or a professional can be helpful in overcoming fear of failure and regaining motivation. Staying committed to our goals and persisting in the face of setbacks can be challenging, but here are some strategies that can help: Set realistic and specific goals: Setting realistic and specific goals can help us stay committed and focused on what we want to achieve. When we have a clear idea of what we want to accomplish and how we plan to achieve it, we are more likely to stay motivated and persist through setbacks.

Create a plan and track progress: Creating a plan and tracking progress can help us stay organized and accountable. Breaking down our goals into smaller, manageable tasks and tracking our progress can help us see our progress and stay motivated. Celebrate successes and learn from failures: Celebrating successes, no matter how small, can help us stay motivated and committed. Similarly, learning from failures and setbacks can help us improve and adjust our approach to achieving our goals. Surround ourselves with support: Surrounding ourselves with supportive people can help us stay motivated and persist through setbacks. Friends, family, and mentors can offer encouragement, advice, and accountability when we need it most. Focus on the why: When we focus on the underlying reasons why we want to achieve our goals, it can help us stay committed and motivated. Whether it's personal growth, career advancement, or improving our health, understanding the why behind our goals can help us stay focused and persist through challenges.

Practice self-care: Taking care of our physical, mental, and emotional health is important for staying committed and persisting through setbacks. Getting enough sleep, eating well, exercising, and taking breaks when needed can help us stay energized and motivated.

Overall, staying committed to our goals and persisting through setbacks requires effort and determination. By setting realistic and specific goals, creating a plan and tracking progress, celebrating successes, learning from failures, surrounding ourselves with support, focusing on the why, and practicing self-care, we can increase our chances of staying committed and achieving our goals.

Here are some steps that can help you overcome fear of failure:

Recognize and acknowledge your fear: The first step to overcoming fear of failure is to recognize and acknowledge that it exists. Be honest with yourself about your fears and how they are holding you back. Challenge your negative thoughts: Fear of failure is often fueled by negative thoughts and self-talk. Challenge these negative thoughts by questioning their validity and focusing on more positive, realistic thoughts.

Create a plan and track progress: Creating a plan and tracking progress can help us stay organized and accountable. Breaking down our goals into smaller, manageable tasks and tracking our progress can help us see our progress and stay motivated. Celebrate successes and learn from failures: Celebrating successes, no matter how small, can help us stay motivated and committed. Similarly, learning from failures and setbacks can help us improve and adjust our approach to achieving our goals. Surround ourselves with support: Surrounding ourselves with supportive people can help us stay motivated and persist through setbacks. Friends, family, and mentors can offer encouragement, advice, and accountability when we need it most.

Focus on the why: When we focus on the underlying reasons why we want to achieve our goals, it can help us stay committed and motivated. Whether it's personal growth, career advancement, or improving our health, understanding the why behind our goals can help us stay focused and persist through challenges.

Practice self-care: Taking care of our physical, mental, and emotional health is important for staying committed and persisting through setbacks. Getting enough sleep, eating well, exercising, and taking breaks when needed can help us stay energized and motivated. Overall, staying committed to our goals and persisting through setbacks requires effort and determination. By setting realistic and specific goals, creating a plan and tracking progress, celebrating successes, learning from failures, surrounding ourselves with support, focusing on the why, and practicing self-care, we can increase our chances of staying committed and achieving our goals.

Here are some steps that can help you overcome fear of failure:

Recognize and acknowledge your fear: The first step to overcoming fear of failure is to recognize and acknowledge that it exists. Be honest with yourself about your fears and how they are holding you back. Challenge your negative thoughts: Fear of failure is often fueled by negative thoughts and self-talk. Challenge these negative thoughts by questioning their validity and focusing on more positive, realistic thoughts.

Set realistic goals: Setting realistic goals can help you avoid the all-or-nothing thinking that often contributes to fear of failure. Break down larger goals into smaller, more manageable steps, and celebrate each small victory along the way. Learn from failure: Failure is a natural part of the learning process. Instead of viewing failure as a reflection of your abilities, see it as an opportunity to learn and grow. Identify what went wrong, and use this information to improve your performance next time.

Focus on the process, not just the outcome: Fear of failure is often focused on the outcome rather than the process. Instead of fixating on the end result, focus on the process of learning and growing. Embrace the journey, and enjoy the small victories along the way. Practice self-compassion: Fear of failure can be incredibly stressful and anxiety-provoking. Practice selfcompassion by treating yourself with kindness and understanding, and remembering that everyone experiences failure at some point. Remember that overcoming fear of failure is a process that takes time and effort. Be patient with yourself, and celebrate each small step forward. With practice, you can learn to overcome your fear of failure and achieve your goals.

III

Lack of Focus

Lack of focus or direction refers to a situation where an individual lacks a clear understanding of what they want to achieve or how to achieve it. It is a state of confusion or indecision that can lead to a lack of productivity, motivation, and progress towards one's goals.

For example, a student who is unsure of their academic goals may struggle to focus on their studies or to identify the best courses or extracurricular activities to pursue. Similarly, a professional who lacks direction in their career may struggle to identify the best opportunities to pursue or to develop the skills and experience needed to advance.

Lack of focus or direction can be caused by a variety of factors, including uncertainty about one's interests or goals, a lack of information or resources, or a fear of making the wrong choices. It can also be exacerbated by distractions, such as social media or other sources of entertainment, that make it difficult to stay focused on one's goals.

To overcome lack of focus or direction, it is important to take time to reflect on your interests and goals, and to identify the steps needed to achieve them. This may involve seeking guidance from a mentor or coach, conducting research, or experimenting with different activities or opportunities. It can also be helpful to minimize distractions and create a structured plan or schedule to stay focused and motivated. With effort and persistence, you can overcome lack of focus or direction and achieve success in your personal and professional life. Lack of focus or direction can lead to confusion and indecision, which can in turn cause a lack of productivity, motivation, and progress towards one's goals. When an individual lacks clarity about what they want to achieve or how to achieve it, they may feel overwhelmed, uncertain, or stuck. This can lead to a lack of motivation to take action or to make progress, as well as a sense of frustration or disappointment.

Without clear goals or direction, it can be difficult to prioritize tasks, manage time effectively, or make decisions that align with one's interests and values. This can result in wasted time and effort, as well as missed opportunities for personal and professional growth.

In addition, lack of focus or direction can contribute to feelings of stress, anxiety, or burnout. When an individual is unsure about their goals or how to achieve them, they may feel like they are spinning their wheels or constantly playing catch-up. This can lead to a sense of overwhelm or exhaustion, which can further undermine motivation and productivity.

Overall, lack of focus or direction can have a significant negative impact on an individual's ability to achieve their goals and succeed in their personal and professional life. It is important to take steps to overcome this state of confusion or indecision in order to stay motivated, productive, and on track towards one's goals.

IV

External Factor

There are many factors beyond our control that can contribute to failure, some of which include:

Economic conditions: Economic conditions, such as a recession or market downturn, can significantly impact business success, often beyond the control of an individual or organization.

Natural disasters: Natural disasters, such as hurricanes, earthquakes, or floods, can cause significant damage to infrastructure and disrupt business operations.

Political instability: Political instability, such as civil unrest or government policy changes, can create uncertainty and make it difficult for businesses to plan for the future.

Technological advancements: Technological advancements can disrupt industries and render certain products or services obsolete, making it difficult for businesses to stay relevant.

Competition: Competition in the marketplace can be intense, making it difficult for businesses to gain market share or attract customers.

Demographic shifts: Changes in demographics, such as an aging population or shifts in consumer preferences, can impact business success.

While these factors are beyond our control, it is still possible to mitigate their impact by being prepared, adaptable, and proactive in response to changing circumstances. By focusing on the factors within our control, such as personal effort, skill development, and a positive attitude, we can increase our chances of success despite external factors beyond our control. Economic conditions can play a significant role in causing failure for individuals, businesses, and even entire economies. Economic conditions can impact the ability of businesses to sell products or services, make investments, or even stay in operation. Some of the ways that economic conditions can cause failure include:

Market Downturns: During a market downturn, businesses may experience decreased demand for their products or services, leading to reduced revenues and profitability. In such a scenario, businesses may need to lay off employees, reduce salaries or benefits, or even shut down operations entirely.

Inflation: Inflation can increase the cost of doing business by raising the cost of raw materials, labor, and other inputs, leading to lower profitability and reduced competitiveness.

Interest Rates: High interest rates can make it more difficult for businesses to obtain financing, which can limit investment and growth opportunities.

Currency Fluctuations: Currency fluctuations can impact the ability of businesses to trade with other countries, which can impact sales, supply chains, and profitability.

Government Policies: Changes in government policies, such as tax laws, trade regulations, or labor laws, can impact the cost of doing business and create uncertainty for businesses.

While economic conditions are largely beyond an individual's control, businesses can take steps to mitigate their impact by monitoring the economic environment, diversifying their revenue streams, and managing costs effectively. This can involve making strategic investments, building strong customer relationships, and maintaining a strong financial position. Natural disasters, such as hurricanes, earthquakes, floods, and wildfires, can cause significant damage to infrastructure and property, disrupt supply chains, and disrupt business operations, which can ultimately lead to failure for individuals and businesses. Here are some ways in which natural disasters can lead to failure:

Physical damage to property: Natural disasters can cause significant damage to buildings, equipment, and other physical assets, which can be costly to repair or replace. This can be particularly devastating for small businesses and individuals who may not have the financial resources to recover from such losses.

Disruption of supply chains: Natural disasters can disrupt supply chains, making it difficult for businesses to obtain necessary materials or deliver products to customers. This can lead to lost sales and revenue, which can ultimately lead to failure.

Business interruption: Natural disasters can force businesses to shut down temporarily or permanently, leading to lost income and customers. This can be particularly challenging for businesses that rely on foot traffic or physical locations to generate revenue.

Loss of workforce: Natural disasters can also impact the workforce, with employees unable to travel to work or forced to deal with personal emergencies. This can lead to reduced productivity and revenue loss.

While natural disasters are unpredictable and often beyond an individual's control, individuals and businesses can take steps to prepare for such events, such as having emergency plans in place, investing in disaster insurance, and having backup systems and redundancies in place. Being proactive in preparing for natural disasters can reduce the impact of these events and increase the chances of recovery and future success. Political instability can have a significant impact on an individual's or a business's success or failure. Here are some ways in which political instability can lead to failure:

Uncertainty and instability: Political instability can create an atmosphere of uncertainty and instability, making it difficult for businesses to plan for the future. This can lead to a lack of investment, reduced consumer confidence, and ultimately, failure.

Economic instability: Political instability can also lead to economic instability, with businesses facing currency fluctuations, inflation, and other economic challenges that can impact their operations and profitability. This can be particularly challenging for small businesses and individuals who may not have the resources to navigate these challenges.

Regulatory changes: Political instability can also lead to changes in regulations and laws, which can impact businesses and individuals. Changes in regulations can require businesses to adapt their operations or change their business model, which can be costly and time-consuming. Failure to comply with new regulations can also result in fines or legal consequences.

Security risks: Political instability can also increase security risks, with businesses facing the threat of theft, vandalism, or violence. This can make it difficult for businesses to operate safely and efficiently, leading to failure.

Overall, political instability can have a significant impact on an individual's or a business's success or failure. To mitigate these risks, businesses can stay informed about political developments, invest in diversification and risk management strategies, and be proactive in adapting to changes in the political and economic environment. While technological advancements have many benefits and opportunities, they can also lead to failure in several ways:

Disruption of industries: Technological advancements can disrupt entire industries, making traditional business models obsolete. This can lead to failure for businesses that are unable to adapt to new technologies or find new ways to compete.

Cybersecurity threats: With the increase in technology comes an increase in cybersecurity threats. Businesses that are not prepared to handle cyber-attacks can suffer significant losses in revenue and reputation, leading to failure.

Dependence on technology: Overreliance on technology can also lead to failure. Technical issues, such as system crashes or hardware failures, can bring business operations to a halt, leading to lost productivity and revenue.

Technological obsolescence: Rapid technological advancements can also lead to products or services becoming obsolete quickly. Businesses that are unable to keep up with the latest technology trends risk falling behind competitors and losing their customer base.

To avoid failure due to technological advancements, businesses must stay informed about emerging technologies and be willing to adapt to changes. Investing in cybersecurity measures, diversifying business models, and developing contingency plans for technical issues can also help mitigate the risks of technological failure. Competition in the marketplace can be intense for several reasons, including:

Similar products or services: When businesses offer similar products or services, customers may struggle to differentiate between them. This can lead to intense price competition, as businesses try to undercut each other to attract customers.

Limited market size: In some industries, the market size may be limited, meaning that there are only so many customers to go around. This can lead to fierce competition for each customer, with businesses fighting for market share.

High barriers to entry: Some industries have high barriers to entry, meaning that it can be difficult for new businesses to enter the market. This can result in a small number of established businesses dominating the market, making it challenging for new businesses to gain a foothold.

Rapidly changing market conditions: In some industries, market conditions can change rapidly, making it challenging for businesses to keep up with the latest trends and maintain their competitive edge.

To succeed in a competitive marketplace, businesses must be innovative, responsive to customer needs, and willing to invest in marketing and advertising to attract and retain customers. They must also differentiate themselves from competitors by offering unique products, services, or customer experiences. Building strong relationships with customers, developing brand loyalty, and consistently delivering high-quality products or services can also help businesses stand out in a crowded marketplace. Changes in demographics can have a significant impact on business success, particularly in industries that rely heavily on consumer spending. Some examples of how changes in demographics can impact business success include:

Aging population: As the population ages, businesses may need to adapt their products or services to meet the changing needs of older consumers. For example, healthcare providers may need to expand their services to provide care for chronic conditions that are more prevalent in older adults.

Shifting consumer preferences: Consumer preferences can change rapidly, particularly in industries such as fashion, food, and technology. Businesses that are slow to respond to these changes may struggle to attract and retain customers.

Diversity: As the population becomes more diverse, businesses may need to adapt their marketing and advertising strategies to appeal to a wider range of customers. This may involve translating marketing materials into different languages, offering products that cater to specific cultural preferences, or hiring staff who can communicate effectively with customers from diverse backgrounds.

Urbanization: As more people move to urban areas, businesses may need to adapt their strategies to reach customers in these locations. This may involve opening new stores in urban centers, developing mobile apps to reach customers on the go, or partnering with delivery services to provide home delivery options.

To succeed in the face of changing demographics, businesses must stay attuned to the needs and preferences of their target customers and be willing to adapt their products, services, and marketing strategies accordingly. Keeping abreast of demographic trends and investing in research and development can also help businesses stay ahead of the curve and maintain a competitive edge in their industry.

V

Negative Self-Talk

Negative self-talk is a common form of negative thinking that can have a significant impact on an individual's mental well-being and ability to succeed. When individuals engage in negative self-talk, they focus on their weaknesses, failures, and shortcomings rather than their strengths and accomplishments. This type of thinking can lead to feelings of self-doubt, anxiety, and depression, and can ultimately undermine an individual's motivation and ability to succeed.

In the context of failure, negative self-talk can be particularly damaging. When individuals experience setbacks or failures, they may engage in negative self-talk, telling themselves that they are not good enough, that they will never succeed, or that their failure is a reflection of their worth as a person. This type of thinking can be self-fulfilling, leading to a lack of motivation, decreased effort, and ultimately, further failure.

To overcome negative self-talk and avoid the cycle of failure it can create, individuals must learn to recognize and challenge their negative thoughts. This may involve developing a more positive and realistic self-image, focusing on their strengths and accomplishments, and reframing their failures as opportunities for growth and learning. Cognitive-behavioral therapy (CBT) is one approach that can be effective in helping individuals overcome negative self-talk and develop more positive and constructive thinking patterns. Additionally, practicing self-compassion, seeking support from others, and setting realistic goals can all be helpful strategies for overcoming the negative effects of self-talk and achieving success. There are many types of thinking that can lead to feelings of self-doubt, anxiety, and depression, including:

Negative self-talk: This involves criticizing oneself, dwelling on one's flaws, and focusing on negative outcomes rather than positive ones.

Catastrophizing: This involves anticipating the worst-case scenario in every situation, even when it is unlikely to happen.

All-or-nothing thinking: This involves seeing things as either all good or all bad, with no room for shades of gray.

Overgeneralization: This involves drawing sweeping conclusions based on a single negative experience, without considering other factors.

Mind-reading: This involves assuming that one knows what others are thinking, without any evidence to support the assumption.

Personalization: This involves taking responsibility for events or situations that are beyond one's control. Catastrophizing is a type of cognitive distortion where a person expects the worst possible outcome of a situation, even if the likelihood of that outcome is low. When catastrophizing, a person may engage in negative self-talk, such as saying things like "I can't handle this," or "I'm never going to succeed." This negative self-talk can reinforce the belief that the situation is catastrophic and lead to increased anxiety and depression.

For example, if someone is worried about an upcoming presentation at work, they may catastrophize by imagining that they will completely forget their presentation, the audience will laugh at them, and they will be fired. This type of thinking can cause them to become overwhelmed and anxious, leading to negative self-talk and self-doubt.

To overcome catastrophizing and negative self-talk, individuals can practice mindfulness, challenge their negative thoughts, and focus on positive self-talk and self-compassion. This can involve reminding oneself that catastrophizing is not helpful, and that it is important to focus on the present moment and take action to address the situation. Seeking support from a mental health professional can also be helpful in learning to manage negative thought patterns.

There is a need to overcome catastrophizing and negative self-talk because they can have a significant impact on our mental health and well-being. Here are some reasons why:

Negative self-talk can lower self-esteem and confidence. When we engage in negative self-talk, we may start to believe the negative thoughts about ourselves, leading to lower self-esteem and confidence.

Catastrophizing can lead to increased anxiety and stress. Catastrophizing involves imagining the worst-case scenario, which can increase feelings of anxiety and stress. This can contribute to physical symptoms such as headaches, muscle tension, and fatigue.

Negative self-talk can lead to feelings of depression. When we engage in negative self-talk, it can reinforce negative beliefs about ourselves, leading to feelings of sadness and hopelessness. Over time, this can contribute to depression.

Catastrophizing can lead to avoidance behaviors. When we imagine the worst-case scenario, we may become overly cautious and avoid situations that could potentially lead to negative outcomes. This can limit our experiences and opportunities for growth and development.

Overall, overcoming catastrophizing and negative self-talk is important for our mental health and well-being. It can help us to build self-esteem and confidence, reduce anxiety and stress, prevent depression, and increase our willingness to take risks and pursue our goals. There are various techniques and strategies that can be used to overcome these negative patterns of thinking, such as cognitive-behavioral therapy, mindfulness meditation, and positive self-talk.

Mindfulness meditation and positive self-talk are two techniques that can be used to promote mental health and well-being. Here's a brief overview of each:

Mindfulness meditation: Mindfulness meditation involves paying attention to the present moment with a non-judgmental attitude. The practice typically involves focusing on the breath or other physical sensations, and observing thoughts and emotions as they arise without trying to control or suppress them. Regular mindfulness meditation practice has been shown to reduce stress and anxiety, improve mood and sleep, and enhance overall well-being.

Positive self-talk: Positive self-talk involves intentionally replacing negative thoughts with positive ones. This can involve reframing negative thoughts, focusing on strengths and accomplishments, and using affirmations or positive self-statements. Positive self-talk has been shown to boost self-esteem, reduce anxiety and depression, and improve resilience in the face of challenges.

Both mindfulness meditation and positive self-talk can be practiced individually or in combination with other techniques, such as cognitive-behavioral therapy or physical exercise. They can also be integrated into daily routines, such as setting aside time for meditation practice or incorporating positive affirmations into a morning routine. While each technique may have its unique benefits, they share a common goal of promoting a positive and healthy mindset that supports overall well-being.

Conclusion

"In conclusion, failure is a natural part of life that we all experience at some point. While failure can be painful and discouraging, it can also be an opportunity for growth and learning. Through examining the reasons why we sometimes fail, such as fear of failure, lack of perseverance, or unrealistic expectations, we can develop strategies for overcoming these obstacles and achieving our goals. By embracing a growth mindset, cultivating resilience, and seeking support when needed, we can overcome failure and move forward with greater strength and determination."

9 798889 864240

Printed by Libri Plureos GmbH in Hamburg,
Germany